T0193350

PHRASE AND WORSHIP

A Spiritual Dictionary for Hope-filled Lovers of Christian Comedy

Donnell "Baby Christian" Owens

iUniverse, Inc.
Bloomington

PHRASE AND WORSHIP
A Spiritual Dictionary for Hope-filled
Lovers of Christian Comedy

iUniverse books may be ordered through booksellers or by contacting:

iUniverse
1663 Liberty Drive
Bloomington, IN 47403
www.iuniverse.com
1-800-Authors (1-800-288-4677)

ISBN: 978-1-4759-4451-8 (sc)
ISBN: 978-1-4759-4452-5 (e)

Printed in the United States of America

iUniverse rev. date: 11/12/2012

IN AN EVER-DARKENING WORLD FILLED WITH SPIRITUAL SPEECH DEFECTS, LET THIS CHRISTIAN AUTHOR/ COMEDIAN BE YOUR LIGHT-BEARING INTERPRETER FOR A UNIQUE LESSON IN THE USE OF SHINE LANGUAGE...

Welcome to the world of Donnell "Baby Christian" Owens – author of this highly unusual "code" book, which explains the meanings of several terms and phrases having bloomed from the flower of his inspirational humor.

So cherish God and salvation – and marvel at these dead-on definitions from a kooky cut-up who creates comic chaos in the comedy club of Kingdom conversion. Happy decoding!

HEALING EVANGELIST/ROVING HOSPITAL PRAYER WARRIOR: *person who has a way with wards*

SPIRITUAL ABSENT-MINDEDNESS: *God's award-worthy device that prevents Him from ever re-visiting your sins from a dead and buried past – thanks to His invention of a tomb machine*

HOUSE OF MELTING IDOLS & CRAZED WORSHIPPERS: *a whacks museum*

UNRAVELING HOLY PARTNERSHIP/PARTING OF THE WAYS: *tragic event that transpires when mistakenly deciding that you and God should take separate vocations*

6-6-6 RETAILER: *defective items you come home with when you purchase your spiritual accessories at BEAST BUY*

DEFINING MOMENTS IN GOD'S WORD:

May the words of my mouth and the meditation of my heart be pleasing in your sight, O LORD, my Rock and my Redeemer.

-- Psalm 19:14

DIMENSION OF TERROR/ HADES HABITAT: *a nightmare on realm street*

WARDROBE OF THE HOLY TRINITY: *a 3-peace suit*

POLLEN OF HUMILITY: *Messianic effect that occurs when a self-righteous person is stung by a humble bee*

DEFINING MOMENTS IN GOD'S WORD:

A word aptly spoken is like apples of gold in settings of silver.

-- Proverbs 25:11

ATHEIST DRAMAS/NERD THEATER OF NON-CHRISTIAN SOCIETIES: *a famous collection of Geek tragedies*

LIMP-NOODLE FAITH: *condition in a non-sturdy spiritual culture that will result in the rise and fall of the ramen empire*

PRAYER: *the umbilical cord between Father and child*

DEFINING MOMENTS
IN GOD'S WORD:

A man of knowledge uses words with restraint, and a man of understanding is even-tempered.

-- Proverbs 17:27

TIME OF NOAH/WATERY PUNISHMENT: *the process of taking a scold shower*

LORD OF THE WORKING & EXECUTIVE CLASSES: *worship of a Loving God who is collar blind*

AVENUE RESIDENT OF ANTIQUATED DARWINISM: *a chimp off the old block*

DEFINING MOMENTS IN GOD'S WORD:

When words are many, sin is not absent, but he who holds his tongue is wise.

-- Proverbs 10:19

SPIRIT-FILLED SINGER: *a music artist specializing in hope-hop*

LUST FOR LOOT/FEAST OF FAILURE: *a bad case of spiritual indigestion resulting from the enemy's constant guarantees that you'll always be seated at the table of wealth – even while he's serving you on pauper plates*

PARTING OF FAITHFUL SOULS AND PIERCING VOICES OF SHARP DISBELIEF: *separation of church and stake*

DEFINING MOMENTS
IN GOD'S WORD:

"...The one who sent me is with me; he has not left me alone, for I always do what pleases him." Even as he spoke, many put their faith in him.

-- John 8:29,30

BLOOD PRESSURE OF AN ANGRY SPIRIT: *correctible condition of a hot-tempered person seeking total peace in Christ – inevitably discovering that what goes up, must calm down*

MESSIANIC ONTAKING OF A TROUBLING CONCERN:
procedure involving a hurt transplant

UNHOLY COFFIN ATHLETES/ SLAM DUNKERS OF CONDEMNATION: *high-scoring team of fallen angels, always hungry to lure lost souls into a sinner-take-all game of casketball*

DEFINING MOMENTS IN GOD'S WORD:

Take the helmet of salvation and the sword of the Spirit, which is the word of God.

-- Ephesians 6:17

SPIRITUAL DELIVERANCE OF VINEYARD DEPENDENCE: *Our Savior's ability to choke off the lengthy stem of severe alcoholism through de-wine intervention*

THE *"I DON'T WANT TO REPENT JUST YET, LORD"* SYNDROME: *a person afflicted with Intention Deficit Disorder*

WINTER MASQUERADE BALL OF THE SOUL: *event for those who claim to be on-fire Christians, but whose cold, snowy hearts are revealed every time they flash their flake I.D.'s*

DEFINING MOMENTS
IN GOD'S WORD:

He replied, "Blessed rather are those who hear the word of God and obey it."

-- Luke 11:28

MEAL OF THE HADES-DWELLING SORROWFUL: *a roast grief sandwich*

MARRIAGE TO CHRIST/ PROMISE OF ETERNAL PARADISE: *a whetting invitation*

7-YEAR TRIBULATION/ SUBSEQUENT IMPRISONMENT OF SATAN: *a sentence at the end of a period*

DEFINING MOMENTS IN GOD'S WORD:

Jesus answered, "It is written: 'Man does not live on bread alone, but on every word that comes from the mouth of God.'"

-- Matthew 4:4

WORRIER IN THE MIRROR/ FEARS OF THE SLEEP-DEPRIVED FAITHLESS: *source material for the movie "STARE WARS: RETURN OF THE RED EYE"*

CELL-PHONE MESSENGERS OF OUR BLOOD-BOUGHT SALVATION: *believers unashamedly committed to the practice of hemo-textuality*

BREAD OF SALVATION/MOUTH-WATERING EDGE TO ETERNITY:
the passion of the crust

DEFINING MOMENTS IN GOD'S WORD:

But the word of God continued to increase and spread.

-- Acts 12:24

BIBLICAL RE-SHADING OF UNHEALTHY SIN COMPLEXION: *healing souls of rebellion ready to dye for the church*

SPIRITUALLY DEVOLVING CIVILIZATION OF PAIN-RACKED BIBLE REJECTORS: *planet of the aches*

RELATIONSHIP WRISTLOCK/ SUBWAY TO HOLY MATRIMONY: *God's plan for Christ-followers riding the singles train to find wedded bliss via couple-tunnel syndrome*

GODLY GROOMER OF PARADISE INHERITORS: *that hot, exclusive "in-crowd" gang – who will become fabulously blessed in the afterlife because they chose the perfect Heir Stylist*

LAST BUT NOT LEAST...

REPENTANCE, *CHICAGO* STYLE: *an action taken by the Windy City author of this book, who realizes that cutting out vices in his life means moving into the spiritual-penthouse apartment at the very top of the SHEARS TOWER*

DEFINING MOMENTS
IN GOD'S WORD:

IN THE beginning was the Word, and the Word was with God, and the word was God.

-- John 1:1

All scriptures taken from the New International Version of the Holy Bible

REPEN *t* ERTAINMENT COMING FROM

THURD/WIRM

MEDIA EUGENICS

www.thurd-wirm.com

WHAT CAN WE SAY ABOUT INSPIRATIONAL HUMORIST "*BABY CHRISTIAN*"?

Nothing his bitter imaginary playmates already haven't. It's been said you won't meet a finer human being on the planet...mostly by junkie parrots being mercilessly exploited in exchange for a cracker fix. In barber school, he was the only student ever to decapitate a practice dummy with an electric beard trimmer. He was so prone to tragedy that as a rebellious teen showing off by smoking in the school bathroom, he accidentally swallowed his tongue while blowing smoke rings. *The Twilight Zone* is changing its name because it's embarrassed he was born there.

But the guy loves God, you definitely gotta give him that!!! And as Christian comedian in-residence at *THURD/WIRM* Christian publishing and entertainment, *Baby Christian* is our *go-to* guy for Grade-A goofiness and sanctified shenanigans! So drop by for a visit with him (read his comedy blogs) at *www.thurd-wirm.com.*

Also at *www.thurd-wirm*.com, check out our other hardback/ebooks for online purchase. Call us at (818) 288-2901 or leave a message for Donnell "*Baby Christian* Owens at *info@thurd-wirm.com.* Follow *Baby Christian* on Twitter/Thurdwirm and catch up with us on Facebook/ Thurd Wirm.

A

THURD/WIRM

MEDIA EUGENICS RELEASE

Printed in the United States
By Bookmasters